P9-CSC-276

ART OF THE MIDWEST — DAVID and AMY Butler

BLUE RIBBON
Food
from the
Farm

RECIPES,

HINTS,

and

HOW-TOS

from the

HEARTLAND

lip smackin'
Jams & Jellies

AMY *and* DAVID BUTLER

with SHARON REISS *and* PHOTOGRAPHY BY COLIN McGUIRE

SOURCEBOOKS, INC.
NAPERVILLE, ILLINOIS

Sourcebooks, Inc.

P.O. Box 4410, Naperville, Illinois 60567-4410

(630) 961-3900

FAX: (630) 961-2168

Copyright © MQ Publications Limited 2001

All rights reserved. No part of this book may be reproduced in any form or by any
electronic or mechanical means including information storage and retrieval
systems—except in the case of brief quotations embodied in critical articles or
reviews—without permission in writing from its publisher, Sourcebooks.

Text copyright © 2001 by David and Amy Butler, Art of the Midwest
Photographs copyright © 2001 David and Amy Butler, Art of the Midwest
and copyright © 2001 Colin McGuire
All rights reserved,
including the right of reproduction in any form.

Design by Art of the Midwest Studio

Printed in Belgium

MQ 10 9 8 7 6 5 4 3 2 1

ISBN: 1-57071-676-5

We would like to take this opportunity to thank our friends and editors at MQP for creating this fantastic series and turning us loose on the culinary countryside! To Ljiljana, for keeping our timelines and waistlines in check, and Zaro, for all the inspiration and good faith! To Colin McGuire for lending his keen eye and out-standing vision to convey such flavor through imagery. And special thanks to Sharon Reiss for joining us in this joyful venture. Her passion for the inherent beauty in culinary and all arts, and the ability to fill our senses with all the good things in life, is all the inspiration we would ever need.

We would also like to thank the farmers, co-ops, and markets which provided us with the fabulous fruits that make up these fantastic recipes. It *all* starts in the hands of the farmer. And for the untold multitude of country cooks—whose creativity and love invite us home with the sweet aroma of a promise kept warm in the oven—we dedicate this book to you.

CONTENTS

The foundation for farm life is "Simplicity."

Why? Try living on a farm. There is never enough time to do everything. So, simplification is key. Buy one pair of work gloves, but don't be cheap about it. Buy a good pair, leather. Boots, same thing. Pull on rubbers that come up to your knees. Hose them off. No time to be fussy. The inherent richness in life is found in the purest forms of its bounty. To expose yourself to that richness, step back from your day-to-day whirlwind of obligation and do something that, with little effort, will reward your senses.

Take, for instance, jam. Fruit, sugar, and maybe a little pectin. Simplicity at its finest. But there are so many variations to explore. So many wonderful hidden tastes. What a fine way to spend a morning on the farm or anywhere you can get ahold of some nice fruit, a few jars, some sugar, and a stove. The aroma, the warmth, and the familiarity rise to the occasion of prefacing a taste. Of which, we think, there is no equal. It doesn't matter which fruit is involved. We've never met a jam, jelly, conserve, preserve, marmalade, butter, or curd we didn't like. And so we exercise!

We live in the country. We've raised many a good-size garden here. Driven the combines, de-tasseled the corn, fed the cows, turned the soil, and picked the berries. We surround ourselves with friends and family to keep us whole and keep us in check. It's a harvest and a sharing community. Ideas, like crops, are traded, given, and kept alive. Every now and then, somebody is driven to writing them down (with so much apprehension). As if it would be tainted in being reduced to "formula." Such is the fate of the recipe. And the most esteemed recipes are rarely written down. They are left to the intuition and the idiosyncratic nature of the cook. Oh, you may want to add some sugar, or, only use blackberries from along the fence on the east side of Yoder's back forty. That's all fine, but we needed a place to start!

So here it is. Between our immediate families and friends we could have filled this book with more recipes than anybody would ever need. But we decided to look outside of our circle, too. We've scoured county fairs, family archives, and arm-wrestled many a little old lady for these recipes. We didn't win all the matches. Most little old ladies are tougher than they look. Sometimes you have to convince the "artist" to share their work with the world. Like so many other things in life, most of the best ones are so simple, yet there is some little element that takes a basic recipe and makes it a Blue Ribbon contender.

We put it all into the more-than-capable hands of chef Sharon Reiss to tweak, test, and weave into this fantastic collection. As an amazing chef and food stylist, Sharon continually shows up with not only the best culinary delights, but inspires us with her presentation. As gifts for holidays or laid out on a platter for improv get-togethers, Sharon presents food to let her friends know how important they are, and that they deserve to be treated like royalty.

Nothing speaks to the heart of inspiration like a great image. And so, along with our own camera foolery, we brought along a true professional in Colin McGuire. He showed us a photograph, a simple piece of strawberry pie. We began to drool. He was hired. A very nice guy and an amazing talent, Colin is used to shooting for "big city" advertising and design budgets. We lured him in with jam! Both Colin and Sharon are living and breathing country air here in the midwest alongside the fields, families, friends, and festivities that we all share.

Amy, Colin, Sharon, and David talkin' jam.

So from here on the farm we send you what we consider to be the best advice, the best hints, some great images, and the absolute best time-tested and true jams, jellies, conserves, preserves, marmalades, butters, and curds the good folks of the country have to offer. It is truly a labor of love. And we start this Blue Ribbon Food from the Farm series in hopes that with each new book you'll find fresh inspiration to rekindle that love of creating, and a renewed desire to make the people around you very, very happy. After all, that's what great recipes are for.

Happy stirrin' David and Amy

GETTIN' STARTED

HAVING FUN

The most important element to this whole thing is having fun. Aside from keeping the area and fruits clean, and the jars sanitized and properly sealed...the rest is just mixin', cookin', and tastin'. We can't stress enough how important it is to work small and don't fuss! Especially when you're just getting started. Some farm cooks will preserve 4 bushels of pears without batting an eye! But to the novice, it would bring only aggravation. Another good tip is to team up. Anytime you have more than one "peeler" or "slicer" it's going to be a better time. Amy and our good friend Nancy Johnson made the most amazing batch of peach jam in Nancy's wonderful farm kitchen and the tag team effort paid off dramatically. We still talk about that amazing batch!

WHAT YOU'LL NEED

Well, Amy and Sharon will tell you that a clean kitchen is in order.

Clear some space and lay out your necessities:

- *deep pans to cook down the fruit and sugar—non-aluminum (non-reactive)*
- *large metal spoons, dippers, and wooden spoons*
- *measuring cup and scales (for fruit, unless premeasured)*
- *spatulas*
- *strainer and/or sieve*
- *jelly bags (or cheesecloth) for jellies*
- *sugar*
- *pectin*
- *fruits*
- *mason jars and lids, labels*
- *a large kettle to boil them in*
- *tongs (for removing hot jars from water)*

- If you want to paraffin the fruit as a seal, either with or instead of a lid, have that around too. It is available as a hard wax (comes in a box) that you melt down. An old tea or coffee pot is handy for this. We'll talk you through that in the canning section.

B00865 528660

What's the difference?

You may not know which one of these preparations to make because you don't know the basic difference between them. That's okay, here's a brief description of each…

Jams—Made from both the pulp and juice of the fruit. A soft, even consistency, generally without the distinct pieces of fruit seen. Bright color and semijellied texture that is easy to spread with very little free liquid. Berries, apricot, plums, and peaches are most common. We start with jams as they are the easiest to make of the group. You basically cook down the fruit and sugar until the right consistency and taste is achieved, and then pour into your jars and seal.

Jellies—Made from the juice of the fruit and set up using its own pectin and/or commercial pectin and sugar. Clear and sparkling with no pieces of the fruit that flavors it. Fruit is cooked and strained to produce the juice and release the pectin. Grapes, apples, and currants are high in pectin and make the most common jellies. Having more steps than jam making—jellies require you to cook down the fruit (usually with water) to pull out the juice, strain the juice through a jelly bag, and cook the juice with sugar (and possibly pectin) until the proper consistency is achieved.

Marmalades—Made from fruits which have jelly-making properties. Jelly in appearance and texture with thin slices of the fruit suspended. Orange, plum, and peach are popular. Made like jelly with fruit slices added at the end.

Conserves—Jam-like consistency made from a mixture of fruits. Frequently using citrus fruits with raisins or nuts. Tender and slightly jelly-like, with little or no syrup.

For Easier, Faster CANNING *use a* **FOLEY FOOD MILL** MASTER SIZE capacity 5 qts.

TOMATOES—With its 5 qt. capacity, the Master Size Foley Food Mill strains bushel into juice in 12 minutes—separates skins, seeds.
APPLES—Mashes bushel into sauce in 18 minutes,—no coring, no peeling. 25% greater yield—delicious flavor—less sugar needed.
STRAINS OR MASHES in half time all fruits for jams, pumpkin, squash, etc. Rices potatoes, strains all fresh vegetables in quantities for family meals.
FOLEY FOOD MILL, MASTER SIZE, at DEPT., HDWE. stores. $4.95

FOLEY MFG. CO., 3372 N. E. 5th St., Minneapolis 18, Minn.
Send canning information Foley Food Mill.

Name ....
(Write address plainly in margin)

Preserves—Whole fruits or larger pieces of fruit cooked in a heavy sugar syrup. Plump and tender with natural color and flavor. Tomatoes and mixed fruits are common.

Butters—Generally made from larger fruits. Fruit is cooked until softened and then run through a sieve or a food mill (or nowadays, a food processor) until given a smooth consistency. Cooked again and thickened with sugar to a spreadable, even texture. Peaches, apples, pears, plums, and grapes make common butters.

Curds—A stirred fruit custard made of eggs, fruit juices, sugar, and usually butter. Unlike jams and jellies, curds are thickened by high-acid fruit juices, protein from the eggs, and heat. A silken texture is accented by the addition of butter. Lemon, orange, and other citrus fruits make common curds.

WHAT TO EXPECT

A mess? Probably. If you're anything like us. Actually, only if you're anything like David. Once the chopping, peeling, and mashing begin, it's hard to avoid. Wear something old! Especially when we're talking about the berry family. You don't want to run screaming for the cold water or laundry detergent right in the middle of simmering some jam. Aprons are a good idea. But really, the mess is minimal if you do it right. Usually the larger the chance for staining, the smaller the fruit, and the easier they are to handle. So that's good.

Expect to improv! Yes, even on these Blue Ribbon beauties. Good recipes are normally good foundations, but your tastes will vary. More sugar, less sugar, maybe the fruit isn't as ripe, more pectin for a firmer yield. You'll get the hang of it. In reality there is only one theme—cooking down fruits and sugar, everything else is merely a variation on that. You can follow these recipes line for line, but realize that they are based on the fruits at hand, and, heck, how will you create your own masterpieces without a little experimentation?

Expect requests. Honestly, it's pretty hard to muck up jams. Even small mistakes can be really, really yummy. Especially if you've got kids around! Jellies and curds require a bit more attention, and certainly no one likes a bitter marmalade: tart, maybe, but bitter...no.

EVERYDAY Canning Terms

Acid Food—All fruits, tomatoes, ripe pimiento peppers, rhubarb, sauerkraut and any pickled product.

Low-Acid Food—In this group are all vegetables (except tomatoes) all meat and other foods that do not fall in the acid group.

Blanch—Bringing the food to the boiling point or boiling for a few minutes then dipping in cold water. Recommended mainly in the preparation of vegetables for freezing.

Precooked—Boiling, steaming, baking or frying for a few minutes before packing food into jars.

Pack—Manner in which food is put into the jar.

Cold Pack—A means of describing the condition of food at the time it was packed into the jar, meaning that it was cold at packing.

Hot Pack—The condition of the food at the time of packing it into the jar. In other words, it has been precooked and was hot when packed into the jar. The hot pack method has replaced the blanch formerly used in the preparation of vegetables for canning.

Head Space—The amount of space left in the top of the jar after packing it with food and liquid. Proper head space is important in retaining liquid in the jar and preventing too tight a pack in foods that expand considerably during processing.

is not sealed by screwing the cap tight. The seal for... as the contents of the jar cool, but the KERR Mas... and KERR Wide Mouth Mason Caps are screwed tig... BEFORE processing.

Adjusting Cap—The manner in which the jar c... is handled or adjusted prior to the time of placing ... into the canner to process.

Processing—The application of heat to food in t... jar to render inactive the bacteria in the food ... sterilize the food.

Method of Canning—This must not be c... fused with methods of processing. The method ... canning refers to the manner in which the food w... packed into the jar; for example, the food may be ... packed or cold packed. These are methods of canni... The open kettle is also a method of canning.

Method of Processing—This refers to t... manner in which heat is applied to the jars of food; ... example, pressure cooker or water bath processing ... a method of processing and not a method of canni...

Venting Pressure Cooker—This term ... being widely used in the place of the former term "... hausting." It means allowing the steam to escape fr... the steam valve of the pressure cooker for a giv... period of time in order to drive the air from the cook... It is a very important step and one which can result... sealing failure or later spoilage if not properly c... ried out.

Exhausting Pressure Cooker—Meani...

DARN GOOD ADVICE and HINTS

As simple and fun as it all is, there's still some basic advice to follow. You'll want to sterilize your utensils (stick them in boiling water) and keep clean work surfaces. Most of what you'll need to know will be handled in the beginning of each section as the questions that arise tend to be specific to each process. But here is some good starting information about stuff that tends to slip through the cracks!

THE FRUIT

You may know your sources and I can tell you that most local farm markets, roadside stands, berry farms, and independent grocers will have some fantastic fruits. But the large chain grocers usually have a good pick of regional finds also. Look for uniformity, and always pick fresh, firm, and ripe fruits. Varieties of fruits (usually based on region) have different qualities, and you should ask the merchants about their characteristics. Most berries will do fine, but there are dozens of apple and pear varieties and a few of them are too bland or too tart for good preserves. Also, they contain different levels of natural sugars, which may affect the amount of sugar you put in the recipe. It's best to start with less and add as you go.

Always work with small amounts—no more at a time than you can do fairly quickly. Follow the amounts in the beginning of each recipe when looking for your fruit. A general rule is that for small fruits (berries and plums) roughly 2 quarts of fruit for 1 quart of preserves, strawberries (a denser fruit) go 3–4 quarts fruit for 1 quart preserves, and larger fruits vary depending on density—apples, peaches, and pears 2 to 3 lbs. per quart of preserves.

Wash all fruits! Just rinse them good in cold water. Remove stems and leaves. Even before peeling skinned fruits. Peaches, pears, and apples should be placed in a solution of cold salt water (2 teaspoons to a quart) after they are peeled to keep them from discoloring. Rinse in cold water afterwards. But if you're making jelly, you will want to cook the fruit without paring or coring to retain and release the pectin.

PECTIN?

If you're new to this whole jelly thing, you might not know what it is! Pectin, acid, and sugar are necessary to produce jelly. They must be of the right kind and in the proper proportion. Pectin is a natural substance found in most juices which causes the juice to congeal when acid is present (in the proper proportion) and sugar is added. Such fruits as tart apples, crabapples, currants, cranberries, blackberries, raspberries, plums, and grapes usually have a sufficient amount of pectin to make jelly.

When fruits lack pectin you can use a commercial brand. Follow the directions on the package. Pectin can also be used in making a firmer jam. We tend to favor a loose consistency for spreading jams and a more homemade taste, and therefore don't use it. Commercial jams bought in stores use pectin to "stiffen up" their product and make it easier to lay out on peanut butter! Follow the guidelines per recipe to see if you need any pectin in your mix. In the beginning of the jelly section of this book, we'll give you a simple test you can use to see if the fruits have enough natural pectin to make jelly.

CANNING TIPS

Canning is not very complicated and only requires that you follow some very basic guidelines. This is the "assembly line" step of the process and you may want (or need) to use a jar funnel, depending on jar size and consistency of product. Follow the tips provided in this section and always, always be careful when handling your boiling water, hot jam, and paraffin!

CONTAINERS

The two most common sizes of jars are I quart and I pint. There are several different brands of mason jars and buying new is certainly our recommendation. If you are using paraffin to seal the jars, then almost any tempered glass that can handle a boiling hot water bath (15 minutes) will do. These are great for gift giving and presentation! For longer term storage we recommend using new jars and two-part metal caps with rubber liners. You may have some glass top containers around, or some other variety, but to ensure a secure, bacteria free product, you'll need to have an airtight seal. This can be achieved with rubber liners, rubber-lined caps, or paraffin.

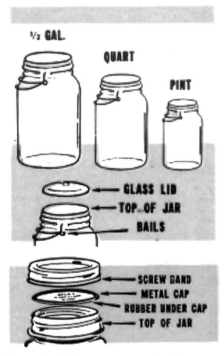

Old bail-top jars are fantastic to look at, but most of them are glass topped, and the rubber seals may be old and brittle. There are new bail-topped jars available at some stores, but be sure to see if they have manufacturers' directions on sterilization. Many discount brands may be unsuitable for canning.

Inspect 'Em

To ensure a perfect seal, the jar top must be smooth and even with no nicks and imperfections. This is a very important step. If the jar doesn't measure up, use it for storing rice or leftovers, but get rid of any jar with chips or cracks in the glass.

To Sterilize

We use the boiling water bath method. It is the preferred method for jams and jellies. Pressure cookers are really only necessary when canning meats and low-acid vegetables that require extra attention to bacteria.

Wash the jars in hot suds and rinse in hot water. Put the jars in a deep pot with a rack on the bottom (to keep the jars off the floor of the pot and keep them from knocking into each other during a rolling boil). Some of you may have a special "water–bath canner" for this purpose. Fill the pot at least 2" over the jar tops and bring to a boil. Cover and cook the jars at a rolling boil for 15 minutes from the point at which the rolling boil begins. Turn off the heat and add the lids. Let the jars and lids stand in the hot water for 10 minutes.

You'll want to time this so that it falls near the finishing point of your product.

Let the cannin' begin

Lift one jar from the hot water with tongs, empty the jar of hot water, and fill it without drying.

Pack tight, but not too tight

Leave a ½" head space for pints and a 1" for quarts. Remove air bubbles by running a clean knife or spatula down the inside edges of the jar. Be sure and wipe the jar neck with a clean cloth to remove any food particles that might interfere with the seal.

Lift both sections of the lid (screw band and metal cap) and screw on without drying. Repeat for all. If you are using separate rubber seals, you can scald them (don't boil them) by placing the desired number of them on a sturdy string and dipping them into the boiling water. For paraffin seals, you'll still need to sterilize the jars in the same fashion.

To paraffin

This is actually a very practical, fun, and elegant way to store your prize. It is especially suitable for small containers given as gifts. It works best on jellies and marmalades, but can be used for jams and conserves, butters, and curds as well. It is not as efficient on preserves where the consistencies are rough.

A small, old-style coffee or teapot is the best tool for melting and applying paraffin. Place the paraffin in the pot and immerse the pot in a pan of hot water over low heat to melt the wax. Pour from the spout onto the top of your product in the jar. If you can, let the jam or jelly mound up in the middle or push down the sides around the jar's inside edges so that the paraffin can creep down around the edges and make a good seal (thicker at the sides). Just be sure to leave

enough room for the paraffin to cover by a 1/4" or more at the top.

If you don't have an old coffee or teapot, you can melt the paraffin in an old pan. Be sure to follow the recommendations that come with the paraffin! It is wax and therefore flammable. Be careful around gas flames and always cook within another pot of hot water to melt.

Cool them off

Place the jars on a folded towel with space between them for the air to circulate. Don't put them in the fridge! Cooling too quickly can adversely affect the seal. Cool at room temperature.

Storage

When the product is cool, pack it into containers or cabinets that will prevent, so far as possible, the entrance of light, moisture, and in-laws! Cooler temperatures are best. It's also wise to use several small containers that will go quickly once opened, rather than larger jars that will need to make repeated trips to the fridge after the first use. Upon breaking paraffin seals, try to remove paraffin pieces from jam or jelly (don't worry, it's non-toxic wax, small pieces won't harm you...but don't eat a big wedge of it) and use either a fitting cap, plastic wrap and a rubber band, or foil. Be sure to refrigerate all opened jars!

Freezin'

You can freeze jams, conserves, and preserves fairly well. Just use the jar packaging as it is shown above, let cool and freeze. When pulling out for later use, don't microwave it, just let it stand at room temperature until ready to use. Jellies, marmalades, butters, and curds do not respond well to the thawing process. One good way to get around that is to make the juice in season and bring it out in the holidays for winter jelly making.

Jams are usually made from the pulp and juice of a single fruit or fruit variety. Berries and other small fruits are the most commonly used. Good jam has a soft, even consistency, a bright color, great fruit flavor and a semijellied texture. In general, use ½ to ¾ pound of sugar to each pound of fruit, or ½ cup to I cup of sugar to I cup of fruit. Crush berries or fruit and cook rapidly without adding water. Stir constantly to prevent burning. Add sugar and cook rapidly until the mixture gives the sheeting test for jelly (see page 36).

JAMS

A.) Use ripe, firm, sound fruit. Sort for uniformity of size and ripeness; work with small batches. Handle gently; work quickly.

B.) The kettle used for making jellies and jams should hold 4 or 5 times as much as the mixture to be cooked. This will allow for a full rolling boil without the danger of boiling over.

C.) Measure sugar accurately. Too much sugar is the cause of many a batch of soft, sticky jelly.

D.) Cook jellies and jams rapidly to retain the natural color and flavor of the fruit, and to make them clear and sparkling. Almost constant stirring is necessary.

E.) To test the jelly, take a small amount of boiling juice in a spoon and allow it to drop from the side. When two partially congealed drops flow together and fall off in a "sheet," the jelly is done. If a thermometer is used, a temperature from

103 degrees C (218 degrees F) to 106 degrees C (223 degrees F) is the jelly stage.

Knox Co. whole strawberry jam

Success starts with INGREDIENTS

4 CUPS STRAWBERRIES
4 CUPS SUGAR
2 TABLESPOONS LEMON JUICE

A country classic recipe from the midwest. Variations come and go, but this is a good foundation.

Wash, drain, hull, and measure the strawberries. In a large, non-reactive pot mix together the sugar and berries. Over a low heat, mix the berries until the juices are released. Raise the temperature. Stop stirring. Allow the mixture to boil at this point for 15 minutes. Do not stir; however, be certain that the mixture is not sticking at the bottom of the pan. Take a wooden spoon and drag it through the mixture. After 15 minutes, the mixture should be set. Pour lemon juice over the top of the berries. When cool, stir in the lemon juice, pour into sterilized jars, and seal.

Yield: approx. 4–5 cups

Jim's prize blueberry/lime jam

Success starts with **INGREDIENTS**

4 ½ CUPS BLUEBERRIES
6 CUPS SUGAR
2 TABLESPOONS LIME JUICE
GRATED ZEST OF 2 LARGE LIMES
3 3-OUNCE POUCHES LIQUID PECTIN

Uncle Jim is not allowed into any summer reunions without a jar. He claims to have invented this recipe, but we think it was Aunt Claire.

Remove any stalks from the blueberries and rinse under cold water. Drain 'em good and put in a saucepan. Crush the berries a bit with a masher. Stir in the sugar, lime juice, and zest. Bring to a boil over medium heat. Keep stirring to avoid burning. When the mix reaches a full boil, cook for 1 minute and then stir in the pectin. Return it to a full boil for another minute.

Place in jars, either paraffin or capped. Cool at room temperature. Keep in a cool, dry place.

Yield: about 6 cups

Indiana bluebarb jam

Success starts with **INGREDIENTS**

3 CUPS FINELY CUT RHUBARB
3 CUPS CRUSHED BLUEBERRIES
7 CUPS SUGAR
1 6-OUNCE BOTTLE LIQUID PECTIN

Rhubarb and blueberries come into season at the same time. One is tart and one is sweet. The perfect combination for a cherished country recipe.

Simmer the rhubarb until tender. Combine with the blueberries in a large saucepan and add sugar; mix.

Place the mixture over high heat and bring to a full rolling boil. Boil it hard for 1 minute while stirring constantly. Remove from the heat and add the pectin. Stir and skim the top for about 5 minutes. Place in jars, paraffin, and cool at room temperature.

Yield: 9 cups

lodger's fig jam

Success starts
with
INGREDIENTS

3 POUNDS FRESH FIGS
½ CUP LEMON JUICE
½ CUP WATER
1 BOX FRUIT PECTIN
7 CUPS SUGAR

Our friend Clarence (85 years old) talked of a lodger that he put up in a room above his garage in 1946. A chef—who provided Clarence with this gift.

Trim the fig stems and chop. Mix the chopped figs, lemon juice, water, and pectin together. Bring to a boil, stirring constantly. Add the sugar to the fruit mixture, return to a full rolling boil, and let boil for 1 minute. Remove from heat. Skim the surface to remove foam. Pour into hot, sterilized jars, and seal.

Yield: about 3 cups

old-fashioned peach jam

Success starts with **INGREDIENTS**

4 CUPS PEELED, CRUSHED PEACHES
5 ½ CUPS SUGAR
¼ CUP LEMON JUICE
1 PACKAGE POWDERED PECTIN

This is the basic peach jam recipe that we follow. If this doesn't get your mouth watering, nothing will!

Combine the peaches, sugar, lemon juice, and pectin; stir well. Bring to a rolling boil and boil for 4 minutes. Stir and skim for 5 more minutes. Pour into sterilized jars and seal.

Yields: approx. 7 cups

spiced peach jam

Success starts with **INGREDIENTS**

4 CUPS PEELED, GROUND RIPE PEACHES
7 ½ CUPS SUGAR
¼ CUP LEMON JUICE
2 TEASPOONS CINNAMON
½ TEASPOON CLOVES
½ TEASPOON ALLSPICE
½ A 6-OUNCE BOTTLE LIQUID PECTIN

Ripe peaches make this such a treat. Great with chicken and pork dishes too!

Combine the peaches and lemon juice.

Add the sugar and spices; mix well. Place it over high heat and bring to a full rolling boil; boil it hard for 1 minute, stirring constantly. Remove from heat and immediately stir in the pectin. Skim off the foam. Cool slightly; stir and skim by turns for 5 minutes. Jar and seal.

Let jam set about 2 weeks before using for best results.

This jam makes for a delightful sandwich spread accompanied by cream cheese or used alone on chicken, turkey, and ham dishes.

Yield: approx. 6 cups

Jerry's pear and apple jam

1 PINT DICED PEARS
1 PINT DICED APPLES
GRATED RIND OF ½ LEMON
JUICE OF 1 LEMON
3 CUPS SUGAR
½ A 6-OUNCE BOTTLE LIQUID PECTIN

Jerry grows pears. They're very common pears but he's convinced they make his recipe sing. He also grows the apples. At any rate, he makes a fabulous jam!

Combine all the ingredients and heat stirring thoroughly until the sugar is dissolved. Add pectin. Boil rapidly until the mixture is thick and fairly clear. Cool slightly and pour into sterilized jars.

Yield: about 1 ½ pints

red raspberry jam

Success starts with INGREDIENTS

8 CUPS RED RASPBERRIES
8 CUPS SUGAR
2 TABLESPOONS LEMON JUICE
2 TABLESPOONS ORANGE JUICE

Tempting to eat before you get the chance to cook them down, raspberries are a true jam favorite. If some are very ripe—that's okay, the pectin will be higher.

Wash and mash the berries. Place in a heavy pot over low heat and cook the berries in their own juice for about 30 minutes, stirring often. Add 2 cups of sugar and bring to a boil. Gradually add the lemon and orange juice alternating with the remaining sugar. Bring the syrup back up to a boil after each addition. When the jam is thick, remove from heat, then jar and seal.

Yield: approx. 8 cups

NOTE:
FOR THIS RECIPE YOU CAN SUBSTITUTE BLACK RASPBERRIES IN PLACE OF RED.

mixed-up berry jam

Success starts with INGREDIENTS

3 CUPS BLACK RASPBERRIES
3 CUPS RED RASPBERRIES
2 CUPS BLACKBERRIES
8 CUPS SUGAR
3 TABLESPOONS LEMON JUICE

Too many berries? Make this wonderful jam.

Wash and mash all berries. Place in a heavy pot over low heat and cook the berries in their own juice for about 30 minutes, stirring often. Add 2 cups of sugar and bring to a boil. Gradually add the lemon juice, alternating with the remaining sugar. Bring the syrup back up to a boil after each addition. When the jam is thick, remove from heat, then jar and seal.

Yield: approx. 8 cups

all-them-basic-berries jam

6 CUPS BLACKBERRIES
    YOU CAN SUBSTITUTE
    BOYSENBERRIES, GOOSEBERRIES,
    LOGANBERRIES, OR BLUEBERRIES
6 CUPS SUGAR
1 TABLESPOON LEMON JUICE

This is a basic formula for berry jams. Any good country cook will tell you to add the sugar gradually, and taste as you go. If the fruit is ripe, you may need less.

Wash and mash the berries. Place in a heavy pot over low heat and cook the berries in their own juice for about 30 minutes, stirring often. Add 2 cups of sugar and bring to a boil. Gradually add the lemon and orange juice alternating with the remaining sugar. Bring the syrup back up to a boil after each addition. When the jam is thick, remove from heat, then jar and seal.

Let stand for a few days to set up before using.

Yield: approx. 6 cups

summer plum jam

Success starts with **INGREDIENTS**

1 POUND PLUMS—DARK OR WHITE
1 CUP WATER
¾ POUND SUGAR

Another juicy summer roadside stand attraction is the flavorful plum. This easy recipe is a favorite of the local county fair circuit.

Clean the plums and cook in water until the skins are tender, roughly 10 to 15 minutes. Cool and remove stones. Add the sugar and heat slowly until the sugar is dissolved. Then cook rapidly until thick. Let cool partially and pour into sterile jars.

Yield: approx. 3 cups

sour cherry/plum jam

Success starts with INGREDIENTS

2 CUPS PITTED SOUR CHERRIES
2 CUPS PITTED PLUMS
1 CUP WATER
¾ POUND SUGAR

You want to take home the ribbon at your fair? Or bring the in-laws to their knees? Make this magical jam. Watch the chores get done!

Clean the plums and cook in water until the skins are tender, roughly 10 to 15 minutes. Cool and remove stones. Add pitted sour cherries. Add the sugar, and heat slowly until sugar is dissolved. Then cook rapidly until thick. Let cool partially and pour into sterile jars.

Yield: approx. 3 cups

Celia's sour cherry jam

Success starts with **INGREDIENTS**

3 CUPS PITTED SOUR CHERRIES
3 CUPS SUGAR
1 TABLESPOON LEMON JUICE

The simplest of the simple. The best ones usually are! A country picnic favorite and especially favored by the kids. Celia never even had it written down.

Crush the cherries slightly and cook until the skins are tender. Add the lemon juice. Cook until the mixture begins to thicken. Add the sugar slowly and cook rapidly until thick.

Yield: approx. 3 cups

farm-fresh apricot jam

1 POUND APRICOTS
1 POUND SUGAR
1 CUP WATER

Apricots are cooked with the skins on—do not remove the skins! The ingredients are simple, but the instructions offer some tips for this delicate fruit.

Wash the apricots and remove the stems. Cut them in half and remove the stones. Place the cut apricot pieces in a large kettle or pot and add the sugar. Add approximately 1 cup of water, or just enough to dampen the sugar. Allow this to stand for 15 to 20 minutes until the sugar has liquified with the water and juices from the fruit.

Put the heat on low and allow to come to a boil, stirring often to keep the apricot skins from sticking (they'll stick to the bottom of the pot if you're not careful). When the fruit starts to boil, keep heat low to simmer.

When the fruit boils, a great amount of foam forms on top. Remove it with a large spoon. Continue to simmer and skim foam every 15 minutes, stirring the jam after every skim. The jam should be cooked for just two hours from the time it starts to simmer. When thick, dollop into sterilized jars and seal.

Yield: approx. 3–4 cups

JELLIES

Good jelly is clear and sparkling and has a fresh, sweet flavor from the fruit of which it is made. Jellies are made from the juice of the fruit only, no pulp. It should be tender enough to quiver when moved, but will still hold angles when cut. Try to make the cooking period of the juice as short as possible since long cooking times reduce the fruit flavor, darken the color, and may reduce the pectin. Again, use the jelly sheeting test! Remember, some jellies take days, even weeks to set up once they are canned. And if it doesn't set up for some reason, Viola!, amazing fruit syrup for breakfast. That's how we discovered our favorite raspberry syrup, and after making so much jelly, we didn't mind at all.

There is an extra step in making jelly that you don't do in making jam. You've got to strain the juices from the fruit pulp. So the first thing you have to do is extract the fruit juice from the fruit by cooking it down.

Extracting Juice

Pectin is best extracted from the fruit by heat, so cook the fruit until soft before straining to obtain the juice. Since pectin is most abundant in cores and near the skins of larger fruits like apples and pears, cook without paring and coring first. Cook juicy fruits such as berries or grapes with no water. Heat slowly until the juices start to flow, then cook more rapidly until soft.

Cook firmer, less juicy fruits like apples and quinces with just enough water to prevent burning. Pour cooked fruit into a jelly bag which has been wrung out of cold water. Hang up and let drain. When dripping has ceased, you may not want to squeeze the bag for the remaining juice, as this tends to cause cloudy jelly.

Homemade Jelly Bags

Use old ham, popcorn, or rice bags of the rough tweed or muslin variety. Wash them well and hang in the sun to dry and bleach. You can also sew up the sides of a piece of white cotton fabric, or use the cheesecloth variety. It's basically a funnel shape that you are adding the cooked fruits into the top of to drain out all of the juice. It may take a while, so you'll want to rig up something to hold the bag over a pot.

Cooking Juice

Long cooking of the juice reduces the fruit flavor, darkens the color, and may even break down the pectin. To make the cooking period as short as possible, cook only 4 to 6 cups of juice at a time and use a pot with a large diameter to provide a large surface for evaporation. When we refer to a non-reactive pot, we mean non-aluminum. Copper or steel works well.

Hints While Cookin' Jelly

Boil sugar and juice rapidly, stirring only until the sugar is dissolved, and then try the sheet test. Take a small amount of boiling juice in a spoon and allow it to drop from the side. When two partially congealed drops flow together and fall off in a "sheet," the jelly is done. If a thermometer is used, a temperature from 103 degrees C (218 degrees F) to 106 degrees C (223 degrees F) is the jelly stage.

Some folks swear by heating up the sugar before adding it to the juice. They say it blends smoother. You can do this by putting the sugar in a 350 degree oven for 5-10 minutes with the door ajar.

Jelly Troubleshooting

<u>Tough Jelly:</u> Too little sugar for the amount of pectin; also overcooking.

<u>Syrupy Jelly:</u> Too much sugar for the amount of pectin; juice too low in pectin or acid, or both.

<u>Cloudy Jelly:</u> Juice not properly strained; slightly overcooked; cooled before pouring; fruits too underripe (too much starch present).

<u>Formation of Sugar Crystals in Jelly:</u> Too much sugar; sugar added too near the finish point of jelly. (If sugar exceeds around 65 percent of the mixture, crystals are likely to form).

<u>Grittiness in Grape Jelly:</u> Precipitation of tartrate crystals naturally present in the grape juice. To avoid this, let the grape juice stand overnight before making jelly. The crystals will collect on the bottom and side of the container; the juice can then be dipped or siphoned off.

<u>*Here's a good old-fashioned test for seeing if your fruit juices have enough pectin to make jelly gel.*</u>

Add ½ tablespoon sugar and ¾ teaspoon Epsom salts to 1 tablespoon extracted fruit juice. Stir until sugar and salts are dissolved and let stand without stirring for 5 minutes. If the mixture sets into a jelly-like mass in that time, the juice contains enough pectin to make good jelly and 1 cup sugar to 1 cup juice may safely be used. If the mass is soft, only ½ to ⅔ cup sugar to 1 cup juice should be used. If the mixture fails to set, add commercial pectin or a juice rich in pectin such as apple or grape.

scented geranium/honey jelly

Success starts with **INGREDIENTS**

2 ½ CUPS STRAINED HONEY
¾ CUP WATER
6 OR 7 ROSE GERANIUM LEAVES
½ A 3-OUNCE BOTTLE FRUIT PECTIN
2 TABLESPOONS LEMON JUICE

Grandma's classic recipe—custom-made for hot biscuits and toast.

Combine honey, water, and 2 or 3 rose geranium leaves; quickly bring to a boil. Add pectin, stirring constantly; bring to a full rolling boil. Add lemon juice and remove from heat. Remove leaves from mixture carefully. Place a fresh, clean leaf in each hot, sterilized jar, and quickly pour hot jelly into them. Seal.

Yield: about 2 cups

Kentucky mint jelly

Success starts with **INGREDIENTS**

2 CUPS PACKED MINT LEAVES, WASHED AND DRAINED
2¼ CUPS WATER
¼ CUP FRESH LEMON JUICE
3½ CUPS GRANULATED SUGAR
¼ TEASPOON SALT
3-OUNCE PACKAGE LIQUID PECTIN
GREEN FOOD COLORING

Mint jelly is not a robust condiment like spicy chutney; however, it can be used to compliment roasted lamb. It's also tasty on warm biscuits with cream cheese!

Crush the mint in a non-reactive, heavy-gauge pot. Use an old-fashioned potato masher. Add the water and bring to a slow boil. Boil for 30 seconds. Turn off heat and allow the mint to infuse the water for 30 minutes.

Pour the infusion through a fine sieve. Measure 1 ½ cups of the liquid and return it to the pot along with the lemon juice, sugar, and salt.

Bring the liquid to a hard boil and add the pectin. Return the liquid to a hard boil and boil for 1 minute. Remove from heat.

Skim off the foam. Add desired amount of food coloring. Green is good! Pour into hot sterilized jars, seal and cool at room temperature.

Yield: 2 cups

honey mint jelly

¾ CUP BOILING WATER
2 TABLESPOONS DRIED MINT LEAVES
2 ½ CUPS STRAINED HONEY
GREEN FOOD COLORING
½ CUP PECTIN

A country favourite for honey lovers. Mint makes it great to eat with afternoon tea and biscuits.

Pour boiling water over mint, cover and let stand for 15 minutes. Strain and add enough water to make ¾ cup. Add honey and heat to boiling, adding coloring to tint a light green. Add pectin, stirring constantly. Heat to a full rolling boil. Remove from heat at once, skim and pour into sterilized glasses. Seal.

Yield: about 6 cups

old-time grape jelly

3 POUNDS CONCORD GRAPES
3 CUPS SUGAR

The only tough thing about making grape jelly can be getting the grapes! Good concord grapes are brimming with pectin and make for a fine Blue Ribbon batch.

3 pounds of concord grapes is around 8 cups, which will produce 4 cups of juice. Rinse, drain, and stem the grapes. Mash them and purée in a food processor or food mill. Pour the pulp into a non-reactive pot and heat. Stir often. Cook until the skins are very soft, about 10-15 minutes.

Pour off the juice, leaving the sediment, and strain through a fine sieve.

Drain in a jelly bag or cheesecloth; allow the juice to drip through overnight in the refrigerator.

Measure the juice. Heat to the boiling point and add ¾ cup of sugar to every cup of grape juice. Boil, stirring to the jelly point. Pour into hot, sterilized jars or jelly glasses. Seal.

Yield: about 2 ½ cups

"no-time" grape juice jelly

Success starts with **INGREDIENTS**

2 CUPS GRAPE JUICE
3 CUPS SUGAR
½ BOTTLE LIQUID PECTIN
1 TEASPOON ALMOND EXTRACT

Ain't got the time to make old-time grape jelly? This quick version of an old favorite is really good too!

Measure the fruit juice and sugar into a large saucepan and mix. Bring to a boil over high heat and add the pectin, stirring constantly. Bring to a full rolling boil and boil hard for one minute. Remove from heat. Add the almond extract and skim the top. Jar and seal.

This recipe can be used with other fruit juices. Check jelly test when making to figure out exactly how much pectin is needed!

Yield: approx. 2 pints

Mae's apple jelly

4 QUARTS TART APPLES, WASHED, STEMMED, AND QUARTERED
2—3 CUPS SUGAR
2 TABLESPOONS LEMON JUICE

A great late summer and fall tradition at Mae's farm. You might want to do the stemming and quartering inside or the bees will give you a fight!

In a large pot or saucepan, add the apples and pour water over them just to cover. Bring to a boil and reduce heat, allow the mixture to simmer. Cook until apples are very soft (about 1 hour). Remove from heat. Mash the apples with a potato masher. Pour the mixture into a jelly bag or cheesecloth. Allow the mixture to drain for 2 hours. Tie the bag together and suspend it over a bowl and allow to drain overnight.

Discard the apples. Add the lemon juice to the apple juice. Measure the amount of juice. Pour the measured juice into a large non-reactive pot. Add ¾ cup of sugar for every cup of juice. Mix. Over high heat, bring to a boil. Boil to jelly test. Remove from heat. Skim off the foam and pour into hot, sterilized jars. Seal.

Crabapples: Use the same recipe as above, but add 4 tablespoons of lemon juice to the apple juice before boiling with the sugar.

Yield: about 6 cups

backwoods sweet cider jelly

4 CUPS SWEET APPLE CIDER
7 ½ CUPS SUGAR
1 3-OUNCE BOTTLE LIQUID FRUIT PECTIN
2 TEASPOONS ALMOND EXTRACT

This may sound like a hillbilly recipe, but that's only because it is! Yummy!

Measure the cider and sugar into a large saucepan and mix. Bring to a boil over high heat and add the full bottle of liquid pectin, stirring constantly. Bring to a full rolling boil and boil hard for 1 minute. Remove from heat. Add the almond extract and skim. Pour into hot, sterilized jars. Seal.

Yield: 9 cups

choice currant jelly

5 POUNDS CURRANTS
SUGAR

With such a short-lived season, currants are a real delicacy in the midwest. Here's a simple way to preserve the flavor for fall and winter.

Wash currants, pick over, and crush. Heat slowly to boiling and boil 5 to 10 minutes, or until currants look white. Strain through a jelly bag or cheesecloth. This may take several hours to get all the juice, you may want to let it go overnight in the refrigerator.
Add 1 ½ cups sugar for every pint of juice extracted and boil until the jelly test is achieved. This should take about 20 minutes. Skim and pour into sterilized glasses, seal with paraffin.

This same recipe can be used for gooseberries and youngberries if they are available in your area. Use slightly underripe fruits.

Yield: approx. 3 ½ cups

Florida's rhubarb jelly

1 ½ POUNDS CHOPPED RHUBARB
1 CUP HONEY
2 TABLESPOONS POWDERED PECTIN

Flo takes such pride in her rhubarb crop that she spends a great deal of time preparing various rhubarb treats during the summer. Here is one of our favorites.

Wash and cut the rhubarb into 1" lengths. Place in saucepan. Add enough water to cook and keep the rhubarb from sticking, but just enough to cover. Cook slowly in a covered saucepan until the rhubarb is soft. Strain the mixture through a jelly bag. Measure 1 cup of the rhubarb juice, add 2 tablespoons of the pectin, and stir vigorously. Bring to a boil. Add 1 cup of honey and continue to boil until the jelly test is achieved. Pour into hot, sterilized jars. Seal.

Yield: 2 cups

all-them-wild-berries jelly

8 CUPS BLACKBERRIES, DEWBERRIES,
LOGANBERRIES, OR RASPBERRIES
2½ CUPS SUGAR

This basic recipe is based on the dark and lovely blackberry, but will work well for almost any small berry variety.

Clean the berries, removing the stems, and rinse in cold water and drain. Take about half the berries, put them in a non-reactive pot, and mash them with a potato masher. Add the rest of the berries whole and set the pot over medium heat. Bring to a boil and stir (use a wooden spoon). Cook thoroughly for 25 to 30 minutes. Stir constantly and don't let them burn.

Remove them from heat and let them cool a bit. Mash all the cooked berries and pour them through a strainer into a bowl. Pour the strained juice into a jelly bag or cheesecloth and let it drip into a bowl or large jar overnight. Measure out the juice and use 4 cups. Put the juice in a wide saucepan and bring to a boil. Add the sugar and stir to prevent caking. Cook rapidly for 10 to 15 minutes and then jelly test. When ready, pour into hot, sterilized jars. Seal.

Yield: about 2–3 cups

Marmalade is basically a hybrid of jelly and jam. It is a jelly base with small slices or pieces of fruit suspended. It has a tendency to appear more cloudy than jelly, but more translucent than jam. It is slightly bittered by the use of zest (citrus shavings) and has a more "discriminating" taste appeal. Still, good marmalades can't be beat, and our country classics show you what happened when these old-world European recipes made it to America's heartland.

We've dispensed with the hints for the following sections to make room for more recipes. They are all variations of jam and jelly, and so, use that same advice here.

country lime marmalade

6 SMALL LIMES
2 LEMONS
5—6 CUPS SUGAR

A rare treat that you can make from store-bought items year round. Makes for a wonderful holiday gift or unexpected treat for guests.

Scrub the lemons and limes, cut them in half and remove the seeds, and then slice them into tiny, thin pieces.

Measure the fruit and juice. You should have about 2 cups all total. Put them in a bowl and cover with 6 cups of water. Soak for 12 hours. In a non-reactive pot, simmer the mixture for 20 minutes. Soak for an additional 12 hours.

For every cup of juice and fruit, add ¾ cup of sugar. Mix all together well.

Cook the marmalade in small batches, 4—5 cups at a time. Boil the marmalade until the juice forms a jelly when tested. Pour the marmalade into hot, sterilized jars. Seal.

Yield: 3 cups

"down south" orange marmalade

Success starts with
INGREDIENTS

2 LARGE VALENCIA ORANGES
2 LARGE LEMONS
3–4 CUPS SUGAR

A classic southern interpretation of the English staple. Ya'll want biscuits?

Wash and slice the oranges and lemons into quarters. Place the prepared fruit and 3 cups of water into a large, non-reactive pot. Bring to a boil and simmer for 10 minutes. Remove from heat. Cool 1 hour and cover. Allow the fruit to sit for 12 hours. Remove the fruit and cut it into small bits. Return the fruit to the soaking water and boil for 1 hour. Measure the fruit mixture. To each cup of fruit mixture add 1 cup of sugar. Boil until thick and jelly test. Dollop or pour into hot, sterilized jars. Seal.

Yield: 3 cups

pear/orange marmalade

Success starts with **INGREDIENTS**

6 WINTER PEARS
2 MEDIUM SIZED ORANGES
3–4 CUPS SUGAR

A fantastic variation on the basic orange. Here's what to do with all that wonderful holiday fruit you have laying around.

Peel the pears and chop. Remove pulp from the oranges and add to the pears. Grind the orange peel and add to the fruit. Measure the mixture and place in a non-reactive pot for cooking. Heat up the fruit mixture. For every cup of fruit, add ¾ cup of sugar. Bring the mixture to a boil, stirring constantly. Cook until thickened. Dollop or pour into hot, sterilized jars. Seal.

Yield: about 3 cups

Here's a great way to show off either of the orange marmalades in this section!

Citrus Platter serves 6–8 people
5 oranges, peeled and sliced
3 blood oranges, peeled and sliced (optional)
3 pink grapefruits, peeled and sectioned
2 white grapefruits, peeled and sectioned
1/3 cup marmalade, warmed

Arrange prepared fruit on a platter. Brush with the warmed marmalade. Garnish with pomegranate seeds and mint.

sour cherry/currant marmalade

1 QUART SOUR CHERRIES
1 QUART RED CURRANTS
1 POUND SUGAR FOR EACH POUND OF FRUIT

Here's one we dusted off of Grandma's archives! This is as basic as it gets and as a result, it's as good as they get.

Wash cherries and pit. Wash currants and remove the stems. Arrange fruit and sugar in alternate layers in a large pot. Cook until thick and clear, stirring frequently.

Yield: about 4 cups

Conserves are jam-like products with a mixture of fruits and occasionally nuts, citrus, and raisins. Use the same tips and hints as shown in the beginning of the jams section. If you're using nuts, they are generally added last when you're just about ready to can.

Preserves are whole fruits or large pieces of fruits cooked in a heavy-sugar syrup. Special effort should be made to keep the fruit as whole and well shaped as possible. Keep 'em plump!

Pre
Cran
F

holiday cranberry conserve

Success starts with
INGREDIENTS

4 CUPS CRANBERRIES
1 CUP WATER
1 CUP NUT MEATS
1 CUP SEEDED RAISINS
2 ½ CUPS SUGAR
1 SLICED ORANGE

A simple recipe for a holiday favorite!

Cook the cranberries in water until they stop popping; rub through a sieve and add the nut meats, coarsely chopped. Add raisins, sliced orange, and sugar, and cook for 15 minutes. Pour HOT into sterilized jars. Seal.

Yield: about 4 cups

Here's a wonderful alternative use for your cranberry conserve.

Omelet with Cranberry Conserve

Prepare a plain, 2-egg omelet and add before folding 3 tablespoons of your cranberry conserve. Garnish each end of the omelet with conserve as well; dust omelet with powdered sugar and brown slightly.

peachy-plum conserve

Success starts with **INGREDIENTS**

4 CUPS PEACHES
5 CUPS RED PLUMS
8 CUPS SUGAR
1 THINLY SLICED LEMON

So much like a fabulous jam, yet the combination of these larger fruits and their size and consistency render it a conserve. What wonderful taste!

Wash, peel, and pit 4 cups of peaches and 5 cups of red plums. Cut the fruit into small pieces and put in a large pot. Add the 8 cups of sugar and one thinly sliced lemon. Stir well into the mix. Boil rapidly while stirring constantly until the jellying point is reached and the mix is thick. Remove from heat; skim and stir alternately for 5 minutes. Ladle into hot, sterilized jars. Seal.

Yield: 12 cups

Gil's raspcherry conserve

1 CUP PITTED CHERRIES
1 CUP RASPBERRIES—RED OR BLACK
1 POUND SUGAR

Gil had all the children convinced there was a fruit called a 'raspcherry' that he bred in his back forty. Although he had no fruit to show, he had his jam.

Clean and stem fruits, pit cherries. Crush cherries slightly and cook until the skins are tender. Add berries and cook until the mixture begins to thicken. Add sugar and cook rapidly until thick. Partially cool. Place in jars, either paraffin or capped. Cool at room temperature. Keep in a cool, dry place.

Yield: 2 cups or about 1 pint

strawberry and cherry preserves

3 CUPS STRAWBERRIES OR CHERRIES
2 CUPS SUGAR

This is a basic recipe for small fruits and can be altered for plums and apricots as well. Any berry smaller than this will just be 'jam' once cooked!

Clean, wash, and drain the strawberries, carefully to avoid crushing. If using cherries, carefully pit. Use whole or cut as desired. To 1 cup of fruit, add 1 cup of sugar. Heat gradually to boiling and boil 6 to 7 minutes. Add one more cup of fruit and 1 cup of sugar. Boil 6 to 7 minutes. Add the last of the fruit and boil for another 6 to 7 minutes. Pour into sterile jars. Seal.

Yield: 3 cups

peach and pear preserves

Success starts with
INGREDIENTS

2 POUNDS PEACHES OR PEARS
3 CUPS SUGAR
2 CUPS WATER

When you buy canned fruits in the store this is basically what you are getting. The difference is in the preservatives, and you'll notice the taste can't compare!

Remove skins from the fruit, cut into halves and remove stones or cores. Boil sugar and water together until the syrup coats a spoon. Add fruit and boil until syrup is thick. Place in hot, sterilized jars. Seal. Paraffin is not recommended with preserves as air bubbles tend to gather near the top.

Yield: about 3–4 cups

BUTTERS *and* CURDS

Fall fruits are falling. Mash 'em up and run 'em through a sieve! It's butter season again. The rich, fragrant colors and tastes of the season are captured fully in these thick, smooth reminders of our heritage preserves. Back in the old days, when fruit started to go overly ripe, this was the "last minute" method for preserving the tail end of the bounty. For farm and city folks who love curling up in a stadium blanket with hot coffee and the morning paper, here is your food.

Curds are associated with our friends across the pond, but are gaining in popularity with American cooks of all ages. Rich and tangy, curds use eggs and dairy and so have a limited shelf life (which is always in the fridge). We know that once you try them, you'll be hooked.

pumpkin-maple-pecan butter

1 29-OUNCE CAN OF SOLID-PACK PUMPKIN
½ CUP WATER
1 CUP BROWN SUGAR
1 CUP MAPLE SYRUP
6 TABLESPOONS FRESH-SQUEEZED ORANGE JUICE
1 TABLESPOON ORANGE ZEST
1½ TEASPOONS CINNAMON
1 TEASPOON GROUND ALLSPICE
1 TEASPOON GROUND GINGER
PINCH OF SALT
½ CUP PECANS, FINELY CHOPPED

Sounds good, doesn't it? It is. And very easy to make once you've added all the ingredients! Easy as pumpkin pie. Well, easier, actually.

In a heavy, non-reactive pan combine all the ingredients except for the pecans. Over medium heat bring the mixture to a boil. Continue to cook until the mixture is very thick. Stir in the nuts, jar, and seal.

Yield: approx. 3 cups

pear-vanilla butter

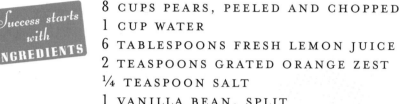

8 CUPS PEARS, PEELED AND CHOPPED
1 CUP WATER
6 TABLESPOONS FRESH LEMON JUICE
2 TEASPOONS GRATED ORANGE ZEST
¼ TEASPOON SALT
1 VANILLA BEAN, SPLIT
1 CUP SUGAR

A great alternative to the famous apple butter. Pear with a hint of vanilla makes for a perfect compliment to rich, malty, multi-grain breads.

In a large, non-reactive pot, add the water, lemon juice, orange zest, salt, and vanilla bean. Bring the mixture to a boil and then simmer uncovered until the pears are very soft. Remove the vanilla bean from the mixture. Scrape seeds into the mixture. Press the pears through a food mill or coarse sieve and add to the liquid mixture. Add the sugar and return the pot to the stove and cook until the mixture is thick. Ladle into hot, sterilized jars. Seal.

Yield: 3 cups

cider-house apple butter

Success starts with **INGREDIENTS**

2 QUARTS APPLE PIECES, PEELED
1 QUART APPLE CIDER
3 CUPS SUGAR
1 TEASPOON CINNAMON
1 TEASPOON ALLSPICE
1 TEASPOON CLOVES

When late summer pushes out and fall rolls in, the late apples drop. We make it a point to come together for a family gathering around this recipe.

In a large, non-reactive pot, add the apples and apple cider. Cook until the apples are tender. Press through a sieve or pass the mixture through a food mill. Add sugar and spices to the puréed mixture. Return the mixture to the pot and continue to cook until it is thick, stirring constantly. Pour into hot, sterilized jars. Seal.

Yield: 3 cups

true-gold peach butter

Success starts with **INGREDIENTS**

4 POUNDS RIPE PEACHES
2 CUPS WATER
2 CUPS SUGAR
¼ CUP LEMON JUICE
GRATED ZEST OF 2 LEMONS
2 ½ TEASPOONS CINNAMON
½ TEASPOON GROUND CLOVE
PINCHES OF ALLSPICE AND NUTMEG

This basic recipe is also good for those "maybe too ripe" plums, apricots, and nectarines, as well. We don't let anything go to waste!

Pit and quarter the peaches. In a large, non-reactive pot, bring the peaches and water to a boil. Reduce heat to low and simmer, stirring often. When the peaches are very tender, run the entire mixture through a food mill or proces-sor until smooth. Return the purée to the pot and stir in the sugar, lemon juice, lemon zest, and spices. Bring to a boil over medium heat while stirring, until the mixture is thick. Pour into hot, sterilized jars. Seal.

Yield: 6 cups

sunrise lemon curd

Success starts with **INGREDIENTS**

1 CUP GRANULATED SUGAR
GRATED ZEST OF 1 LEMON
½ CUP FRESH-SQUEEZED LEMON JUICE
[DO NOT USE BOTTLED LEMON JUICE]
4 WHOLE EGGS AND 1 EXTRA EGG YOLK
10 TABLESPOONS UNSALTED BUTTER

Farm-fresh eggs and real lemon juice make this curd the blue ribbon recipe that it is. Be sure to refrigerate after making and serve cooled or at room temperature.

Mix the sugar and lemon zest together. Cut the butter into 1" pieces.
In a non-reactive saucepan, add the lemon juice, eggs, egg yolk, butter, and the lemon zest/sugar mixture. Combine. Over medium heat cook the mixture for 4–5 minutes, stirring constantly. Cook until the mixture is thickened. Remove the pan from heat before the mixture comes to a boil. Pour through a sieve into a bowl. Cover the top of the curd with a piece of plastic wrap to avoid a skin from forming, or if you desire, jar and seal in sterilized jars. Curd will hold for 1 week in the refrigerator or it can be frozen for up to 2 months. Defrost in the refrigerator overnight.

Yield: approx. 1 quart

e-z three-citrus curd

Success starts with INGREDIENTS

4 LARGE EGG YOLKS
10 TABLESPOONS SUGAR
2 TABLESPOONS LEMON JUICE
1 TABLESPOON LIME JUICE
2 TABLESPOONS FRESH ORANGE JUICE
4 OUNCES BUTTER
2 TEASPOONS ORANGE ZEST

You may have the makings for this one in the refrigerator right now. Using only juices, eggs, sugar, butter, and the zest of one orange you can make a tangy, fresh curd!

In a medium-sized, non-reactive saucepan, mix together the eggs and sugar. (Mixing together the sugar and yolks before adding the juice will help to prevent the mixture from curdling.) Whisk together for 1 minute. Cut the butter into 1" pieces. Add the juices and butter to the sugar/egg mixture. Over a medium heat, stir until it begins to thicken. Continue to cook until just short of the boiling point. The mixture should no longer look translucent, it will be opaque. Remove from heat and pour through a sieve. Fold in the orange zest. Cover the curd with plastic wrap and chill. You can also place in sterilized jars and seal. This will keep in the refrigerator for 3 weeks or it can be frozen for up to 3 months. Defrost in the refrigerator overnight.

Yield: approx. 2 cups

limelight-island curd

Success starts with
INGREDIENTS

1 CUP GRANULATED SUGAR
GRATED ZEST OF 1 LIME
¼ CUP FRESH-SQUEEZED LIME JUICE
¼ CUP FRESH-SQUEEZED LEMON JUICE
[DO NOT USE BOTTLED LEMON JUICE]
4 WHOLE EGGS AND 1 EXTRA EGG YOLK
10 TABLESPOONS UNSALTED BUTTER
PINCH OF NUTMEG
2 TABLESPOONS COCONUT MILK

Feeling exotic? This is about as crazy as we get here in the country. Now don't go adding any rum to this concoction! Best eaten on a hammock.

Mix the sugar, nutmeg, and lime zest together. Cut the butter into 1" pieces. In a non-reactive saucepan, add the lemon and lime juice, eggs, egg yolk, butter, and the lemon zest/sugar mixture. Combine. Over medium heat cook for 4–5 minutes, stirring constantly. Add the coconut milk. Cook until the mixture is thickened. Remove the pan from heat before the mixture comes to a boil. Pour through a sieve into a bowl. Cover the top of the curd with a piece of plastic wrap to avoid a skin from forming, or if you desire, jar and seal in sterilized jars. Curd will hold for 1 week in the refrigerator or it can be frozen for up to 2 months. Defrost in refrigerator overnight.

Yield: approx. 1 quart

BREADS FOR SPREADIN'

Hey, what a swell idea! Once we got into developing this book, we realized that great jam on not-so-great breads and biscuits is a shame (and maybe a waste of good jam). So we researched, poked, and prodded some folks to give up their absolute best bedding for our jams and jellies. You wouldn't drink fine wine out of a plastic cup, would you? A blue ribbon jam deserves no less than a blue ribbon bread!

orange-marmalade nut bread

Success starts with INGREDIENTS

3 CUPS ENRICHED FLOUR

1 TABLESPOON BAKING POWDER

¾ TEASPOON SALT

¼ CUP SUGAR

½ CUP ORANGE MARMALADE

2 TABLESPOONS GRATED ORANGE RIND

¼ CUP SHORTENING

1 EGG, WELL BEATEN

1 CUP MILK

1 CUP NUT MEATS

The marmalade is great. This bread is no slouch either! Spread with more marmalade, orange, or other, for a break from the same old bread.

Mix together the flour, baking powder, salt, sugar, and grated orange rind. Cut in the shortening with 2 knives or a pastry blender—the mixture should resemble a fine cornmeal. Mix the egg and milk together and add the orange marmalade. Add this wet mixture to the dry and mix slowly until incorporated. Do not overmix! Add nuts and mix a bit more until incorporated. Pour into a well-greased loaf pan about 10 x 5 x 3 ½ inches. Let stand for 20 minutes and then bake. Bake at 350 degrees for 45–50 minutes.

Sharon's cream biscuits

Success starts with INGREDIENTS

2 CUPS ALL-PURPOSE FLOUR

1 TEASPOON SALT

1 TABLESPOON BAKING POWDER

2 TEASPOONS SUGAR

1 CUP PLUS 2 TABLESPOONS HEAVY CREAM

⅓ CUP UNSALTED BUTTER, MELTED

Yep. Our own Sharon devised these amazing cream beauties (seen on the intro page of this section). A mouth-watering biscuit even without jam!

Preheat oven to 425 degrees. Mix the flour, salt, baking powder, and sugar in a mixing bowl. Add the cream to the dry ingredients and mix. Gather the dough together and knead a few times in the bowl. The dough should feel tender. On a lightly floured surface, knead for 1 additional minute. Pat the dough into a ½" thick square and cut into 12 pieces. Place biscuits on an ungreased cookie sheet. Brush the tops of the biscuits with the melted butter. Bake for 15–17 minutes or until light golden brown.

currant cream scones

Success starts with INGREDIENTS

2 CUPS ALL-PURPOSE FLOUR
1 TABLESPOON BAKING POWDER
½ TEASPOON SALT
½ CUP DRIED CURRANTS, SOAKED IN WARM WATER FOR 5 MINUTES, AND DRAINED

1 ¼ CUP HEAVY CREAM
¼ CUP SUGAR

GLAZE: 4 TABLESPOONS UNSALTED BUTTER, MELTED
2 TABLESPOONS COARSE SUGAR

Heaven in a half-circle. Fantastic for tasting parties!

Preheat oven to 425 degrees. Mix the flour, baking powder, salt, and sugar in a mixing bowl. Add the drained currants. Stir in the cream and mix the dough until it holds together in a mass. On a lightly floured surface, knead the dough 4–5 times. Form the dough mass into an 8–10" circle. Place the circle on an ungreased cookie sheet. Brush the top surface with the melted unsalted butter and sprinkle coarse sugar on top. Mark the dough into wedges by cutting only halfway through the dough. Bake for 15–17 minutes or until golden brown. Cool for 5 minutes and pull the circle apart into the formed wedges, or serve as a half-circle for guests to break (shown).

grandma's soda biscuits

Success starts with INGREDIENTS

2 CUPS ALL-PURPOSE FLOUR
½ TEASPOON BAKING SODA
¼ TEASPOON SALT
4 TABLESPOONS SHORTENING
¾ CUP SOURED MILK OR BUTTERMILK

Soda? As in baking soda. We didn't ask grandma dumb questions when she was baking. We just got out of the way. These were her favorites.

Sift the flour and then measure it. Sift in the baking soda and salt. Cut shortening into the dry ingredients until it is as fine as coarse cornmeal. To sour the ¾ cup of milk artificially and quickly, place 1 tablespoon of lemon juice or white vinegar in a measuring cup, add milk, and mix well.

Add enough of the milk to make a soft dough. This may take 1 tablespoon more or less milk, so go slowly. Turn the dough on a floured surface, knead slightly. Roll ½" thick and cut with a floured biscuit cutter. Prick with a fork.

Place biscuits on an ungreased baking sheet and bake in a preheated 475 degree oven for 10–12 minutes. Makes about 12 biscuits.

peanut butter "preserve-prints"

Success starts with INGREDIENTS

½ CUP UNSALTED BUTTER
½ CUP LIGHT BROWN SUGAR
½ CUP GRANULATED SUGAR
1 CUP FAVORITE PEANUT BUTTER
1 LARGE EGG
½ TEASPOON VANILLA

1 CUP ALL-PURPOSE FLOUR
1 TEASPOON BAKING SODA
⅛ TEASPOON SALT

12 OUNCES SOUR CHERRY
OR STRAWBERRY PRESERVES

These cookies are a national treasure. Chances are you've had them. If not, make them! Use whatever flavor you like, but sour cherry and strawberry are sure bets!

Preheat oven to 375 degrees. In a mixing bowl, cream the butter. Add the sugars and beat until mixed. Add the peanut butter and beat for 1 minute. Mix the egg and vanilla together and add to the butter mixture. Beat until incorporated. Scrape the sides of the bowl to ensure even mixing. Mix together the flour, soda, and salt. Add the dry ingredients to the batter, and on low speed mix until all of the flour is incorporated. Refrigerate the dough for 1–2 hours. Scoop cookie dough balls (about 2 tsp. in size), and roll to form 1" balls. Place balls on ungreased cookie sheets, about 2 inches apart from each other. Make indentations with a spoon or your finger in the center of each cookie. Bake for 10–12 minutes or until light golden in color. Place the cookies on a cooling rack, and prepare the preserves. Heat the preserves and strain. Place cherries or strawberries in the center of the cookies. The remaining juice should be reduced by boiling for about 3–5 minutes. Cool the thickened juice for 1 minute then spoon over the top of the fruit.

Store cookies in an airtight container, single layer of cookies.

COMPLIMENTS OF

Friends that are cooks would love a measuring cup full of apple jelly. Antique collectors, new neighbors, and kids of all ages smile wide when holding a comical glass full of clear jelly!

FROM THE HEART

GIFT GIVING IDEAS

If you're going to make homemade jam or jelly, isn't it worth showing off? Sure! A big part of the fun of making your own home recipes is giving them away to friends and family. With a little creative thinking, you can turn some inexpensive jams and jellies into wonderful presents and presentations that will keep on giving after the jam sessions are over. As long as you can sanitize the container, using paraffin or a sealable cap, you can explore many variations.

Use the paraffin to your advantage. Kids love surprises embedded in the warm wax and the jelly that lies beneath! Works well for antique lovers too.

Portraits of a loved one, maybe the recipe creator. If you don't want to give up the photo, make a color copy and mount it onto board. Great for families during the holidays or on special occasions.

Fancy vintage tags, like this card tally, make unique flavor markers!

Wrapped in complimentary ribbon. Let the light shine in! Especially effective with vintage ribbons and accents (like these fabric flowers).

Something as simple as a piece of newspaper under the rim of a standard mason jar can make for an elegant and warm wrap.

Old fabric and a large mailing label clearly identifies this as a gift especially made for someone special.

Quilt squares are still a popular and classic way to wrap your prize jam. Tie off with jute.

Country cooks will love to get the gift that keeps on giving in this measuring cup filled with apple jelly.

111

If you can find them, vintage labels mixed with a wonderful old jar alone can become a simply beautiful presentation.

BLACKBERRY